SPIRITUAL BABY

BUILDING VALUES EARLY

RUKMINI SREENIVASAN

TRANSLATED BY

ANU RANGANATH

INDIA · SINGAPORE · MALAYSIA

Notion Press

Old No. 38, New No. 6
McNichols Road, Chetpet
Chennai - 600 031

First Published by Notion Press 2020
Copyright © Rukmini Sreenivasan, Anu Ranganath 2020
All Rights Reserved.

ISBN 978-1-64783-555-2

This book has been published with all efforts taken to make the material error-free after the consent of the author. However, the author and the publisher do not assume and hereby disclaim any liability to any party for any loss, damage, or disruption caused by errors or omissions, whether such errors or omissions result from negligence, accident, or any other cause.

While every effort has been made to avoid any mistake or omission, this publication is being sold on the condition and understanding that neither the author nor the publishers or printers would be liable in any manner to any person by reason of any mistake or omission in this publication or for any action taken or omitted to be taken or advice rendered or accepted on the basis of this work. For any defect in printing or binding the publishers will be liable only to replace the defective copy by another copy of this work then available.

Contents

Acknowledgements   5

Praying with a Purpose   7

1. Bedtime prayer to be chanted before going to bed   8
2. Arjuna Shloka   9
3. Kartha Veeryarjuna   10
4. Shloka while giving bath to a baby boy   11
5. Shloka while giving bath to a baby girl   12
6. Prayer to the Banyan Tree   13
7. Prayer to Bilva Tree   14
8. Prayer to Avoid Kali Yuga Influence   15
9. Prayer to Chant During a Bath   16
10. Prayer for New Beginnings (During Ugadi Festival)   17
11. Prayer While Lighting the Lamp   18
12. Morning Prayer   19
13. Prayer Before Starting a Journey   20

One Prayer for Every God   21

14. Lord Ganesha   22
15. Guru Prayer   23
16. Lord Vishnu   24
17. Goddess Lakshmi   25

18. Goddess Sharade	26
19. Nava Graha Prayer	27
20. Thulasi Prayer	28
21. Prayer to the Moon	29
22. Mother Annapoorna	30
23. Prayer to the Lamp	31
24. Gayatri Mantra	32
25. Lord Dakshinamurthy	33
26. Lord Hanuman	34
27. Lord Hayagreeva	35
28. Vyasa Prayer	36
29. Goddess Saraswati	37
30. Lord Krishna	38
31. Lord Rama	39
32. Lord Venkateswara	40
33. Panchayudha Prayer	41

ACKNOWLEDGEMENTS

Putting a book together is harder than I thought and more rewarding than I could have ever imagined. None of this would have been possible without my mother. From reading early drafts to giving me advice on the cover to keeping the munchkin out of my hair so I could edit, she was as important to this book getting done as I was. Thank you so much, Amma.

I'm eternally grateful to my sister and brother-in-law, Swetha and Akshay, for always being there for me. Thanks, Swe and Akshay.

This book wouldn't have been possible without my grandmother, who taught me the prayers and to stay positive always. Thanks, Pati.

To my loving husband, Sandeep, who is supportive of everything I do. Thanks, Sand.

To my late father, who is always missed and was wonderful. Thanks, Appa.

Finally, to all my wonderful friends and family, thank you all.

Thanks to Notion Press for making this journey smooth.

Praying with a Purpose

Bedtime prayer to be chanted before going to bed

Purpose:

Praying for a peaceful sleep.

Prayer:

Ramaskandam Hanumantham Vynatheyam Vrukodharam

Sayanesha Smarenithyam Dhuswapnam Thasya Nashyathi

Arjuna Shloka

Purpose:
To overcome fear during thunder and lightning.

Prayer:
Arjuna Phalguna Partha Keerita Shwethavahana
Bhibhatsura Vijayi Krishna Savyasachi Dhanenjaya

Kartha Veeryarjuna

Purpose:

To recover lost things.

Prayer:

Om Karthaveeryarjuno nama Raja baahu sahasravan

Thasya smarana mathrenaGatham nashtam cha labhyathe

Shloka While Giving Bath to a Baby Boy

Purpose:
Recalling the immortals while giving a bath to a baby boy.

Prayer:
Aswatthama Balir Vyaso Hanumanashcha Vibhishana
Krupacharyacha Parashurascha Saptaitey Chirjeevan

Shloka while giving bath to a baby girl

Purpose:

Recalling the goddesses while giving a bath to a baby girl to provide strength and to get rid of sins and ill feelings.

Prayer:

Ahalya Draupadi Kunti Tara Mandodari tatha

Panchakanyeh smarennityam mahapatakakanasinih

Prayer to the Banyan Tree

Purpose:

Ashwata tree is the most sacred tree. Even gods offer prayers to this 'Lord of all trees.'

Prayer:

Moolatho Brahma roopaya, madhyatho Vishnu roopine,
Agratha shiva roopaya Vruksha rajaya they nama

Prayer to Bilva Tree

Purpose:
A powerful chant that speaks of the power and glory of offering Bilva leaves to Lord Shiva.

Prayer:
Tridalam trigunakaram trinetram cha triyayudham
Trijanmapapasamharam ekabilvam shivarpanam

Prayer to Avoid Kali Yuga Influence

Purpose:

To avoid 'Kali' interference in daily deeds.

Prayer:

Karkotakasya Nagasya Damiyamtyaha Nalasyacha
Rituparnasya RajaRishi Keertanam Kalinashanam

Prayer to Chant During a Bath

Purpose:
Invoking the presence of holy water.

Prayer:
Gange cha yamune chaiva godavari saraswathi
narmade sindhu kaveri jalesmin sannidhim kuru

Prayer for New Beginnings (During Ugadi Festival)

Purpose:

Life is both bitter and sweet; embrace it as it comes.

Prayer:

Shatayur Vajra Dehaya Sarva Sampath Karayacha

SarvarisTa Vinashaya Nimbakam dhaLa BhakshaNam

Prayer While Lighting the Lamp

Purpose:

While lighting lamps or turning on the light in the evening.

Prayer:

Deepam Jyothi Parabramham

Deepam Sarva Tamopaham

Deepena Saadhyathe Sarvam

Sandhya Deepam Namosthuthe

Morning Prayer

Purpose:

Prayer to the three Tattvas of Wealth, Wisdom and Power at the beginning of the day.

Prayer:

Karagre Vasate Laxmi Karmadhye Saraswati

Karamule Tu Govindha Prabhate Kardarshanam

Prayer Before Starting a Journey

Purpose:

Prayer to protect us from any danger and to make our journey smooth.

Prayer:

Vanamali Gadi Sharangee Changee chakreecha Nandaki

Sriman NarayanoVishnurVasudevobi Rakshatu

One Prayer for Every God

Lord Ganesha

Purpose:

"Vighneshwara" is the Conqueror of Obstacles.
This is a Stotra in praise of him, praying to remove the obstacles on our path.

Prayer:

ShuklaAmbara Dharam Vishnum Shashi
Varnam Chatur Bhujam

Prasanna Vadanam Dhyaayet Sarva Vighnopashaantaye

Guru Prayer

Purpose:

Prayer bowing to the creator, preserver and destroyer.

Prayer:

GururBrahma GururVishnu GururDevo Maheshwaraha

Guru Saakshaat ParaBrahma Tasmai Sri Gurave Namaha

Lord Vishnu

Purpose:

Salutations to the lord of all lokas.

Prayer:

Shaanta-Aakaaram Bhujaga-Shayanam
Padma-Naabham Sura-Iisham

Vishva-Aadhaaram Gagana-Sadrsham
Megha-Varnna Shubha-Anggam

Lakssmii-Kaantam Kamala-Nayanam
Yogibhir-Dhyaana-Gamyam

Vande Vissnnum Bhava-Bhaya-Haram
Sarva-Loka-Eka-Naatham

Goddess Lakshmi

Purpose:

Salutations to the Goddess of all wealth, money and richness.

Prayer:

Lakshmi Ksheera Samudra Raaja Tanaya
Sree Ranga Dhaameshvari

Daasi Bhootha Samasata Deva Vanithaam
Lokaika Deepankuram

Sreeman Manda Kataaksha Labdha Vibhava
Brahmendra Gangaadharam

Tvaam Trailokya Kudumbineem Sarasijam
Vande Mukunda Priyaam

Goddess Sharade

Purpose:

Prayer to give us the gift of education and knowledge.

Prayer:

Namaste sharada devi Kashmira puravaasini
twamaham prarthate nityam vidyam lakshmincha dehime

Nava Graha Prayer

Purpose:

Chanting this stotra can liberate us from all sins and ill effects that may occur due to planetary positions.

Prayer:

Om Namah Sooryaya Chandraya Mangalaya Budhaya Cha

Guru Shukra Shanibhyascha Raahave Ketave Namo Namaha

Thulasi Prayer

Purpose:
Prayers to the holy Tulasi in whose stem all the Gods reside and in whose leaves the Vedas reside.

Prayer:
Yanmule sarva thirthani yanmadye sarva devatha
yadagre sarva vedashcha Tulasi thvam namam mayham

Prayer to the Moon

Purpose:
Seeking emotional stability and sensitivity.

Prayer:
Ksheera saagar Sambhoota Lakshmi devi sahodara
Neela kantha Jatha jhoota balachandra Namostute

Mother Annapoorna

Purpose:

To awaken within me Spiritual Knowledge and Freedom from all Worldly Desires.

Prayer:

Annapurne sadaa purne, Sankara praana vallabhe,
Jnana vairagya sidhyartham,
Bikshaam dehee cha parvathy

Prayer to the Lamp

Purpose:

Salutations to the Light of the Lamp for Auspiciousness, Health and Prosperity.

Prayer:

Shubham karoti kalyaanam aarogyam dhana sampadaa

Shatru buddhi vinaashaaya deepa jyothir namostute

Gayatri Mantra

Purpose:

Gayatri Mantra is a complete prayer for protection, nourishment and finally, liberation.

Prayer:

Om bhoor bhuvah svah Tat savitur varenyam

bhargo devasya deemahi dhiyo yo nah prachodayaat

Lord Dakshinamurthy

Purpose:

Lord Dakshinamurthy is a powerful Avatar of the Hindu God, Shiva, who appears as a Guru (teacher) to guide one on the right path.

Prayer:

Om Namah Pranna vaarthaaya Shuddha
Jnyaanaika-Muurtaye
Nirmalaaya Prashaantaaya Dakssinna muurtaye Namah

Lord Hanuman

Purpose:

Hanuman prayer is beneficial in fulfilling the genuine wishes of people. It confers wealth, health, prosperity and happiness on those who chant it with due reverence and concentration.

Prayer:

Mano Javam Maaruta Tulya Vegam Jitendriyam Buddhi Mataam Varissttham

Vaatatmajam Vaanara Yuutha Mukhyam ShriiraamaDuutam Sharannam Prapadyeth

Lord Hayagreeva

Purpose:
Salutations to Lord Hayagreeva, who is the embodiment of Sri Maha Vishnu.

Prayer:
Jnananandamayam devam nirmala sphatikakrutim,
aadharam sarvavidyaanaam Hayagreevamupasmahe

Vyasa Prayer

Purpose:

Offering respects to Vyasa, who is free from all defects and is a treasure of austerities.

Prayer:

Vyasam Vasishta naptaram sakteh pautrama kalmasham
parasaratmajam vande Sukatatam tapo nidhim

Goddess Saraswati

Purpose:

Salutations to the Goddess of learning, wisdom, speech and music.

Prayer:

Ya Kundendu Tusharahara Dhavala
Ya Shubhra Vastravrita

Ya Veena Varadanda Manditakara
Ya Shveta Padmasana

Ya Brahmachyuta Shankara Prabhritibihi
Devaih Sada Pujita

Sa Mam Pattu Saravatee Bhagavatee Nihshesha Jadyapaha

Lord Krishna

Purpose:

Worship to Lord Krishna, the spiritual master of the universe.

Prayer:

Vasude Vasutam devam Kamsa Chanoora mardhanam

Devaki Paramanandam Krishnam Vande Jagatgurum

Lord Rama

Purpose:

One who approaches Sri Rama with love becomes wide in heart, pure in spirit and good in nature.

Prayer:

Ramaya Ramabadhraya Ramachandraya Vedhase
Raghunathaya nathaya Seeta pataye namaha

Lord Venkateswara

Purpose:

Praying to Lord Venkateswara to grant all legitimate demands of his disciples in the Kali Yuga.

Prayer:

Sriyah kanthaya kalyana nidhaye nidhayerthinam

Sri Venkata nivasaya Srinivasaya Mangalam

PANCHAYUDHA PRAYER

Purpose:

This prayer is addressed to the five weapons of Lord Vishnu, viz

Holy wheel (Sudarshana),

Conch (Pancha Janya),

Mace (Gomodhakee),

Sword and

Bow (Sarngam).

They are considered to be great sages in the service of Lord Vishnu

Prayer:

Sphurad sahasrara Shikhadhi theevram
Sudarshanam Bhaskara koti thulyam

Suradvisham prana vinasi vishno
Chakram Sadaham saranam prapadhye

Vishnor mkhothonila poorithasya
Yasya dwanir Dhanava dharpa hantha

Tham Pancha janyam, sasi koto shubhram
Sankham sadaham saranam Prapadhye

Hiranmayim Meru samana saram
Koumodhakeem daithya kulaika hanthrim

Vaikunta vamagra karabhimrushtam
Gadham sadaham saranam prapadhye

Raksho uraanaam katinogra kanadach
Chethakshara sonitha digdha dhaaraam

Tam Nandakam nama Hare pradeeptham
Gadgam sadaham saranam prapadhye

Ya jjayani nadha sravanath suraanam
Chethamsi nirmuktha bhayani sadhya

Bhavanthi daithyasani bana varsha
Sarngam sadaham, saranam prapadhye